Think What You Want

An Adaptation of James Allen's
As a Man Thinketh

Bruce Lee Whitney

Monarch Unlimited
Los Angeles, CA

Copyright © 2015 by Bruce Lee Whitney

All rights reserved. This book or any portion thereof may not be reproduced or used in any manner whatsoever without the express written permission of the publisher except for the use of brief quotations in a book review.

Original version, *As a Man Thinketh*, copyright © 1904 by James Allen

Cover design by Ed Ward / Mental-Ward.com
Book Layout ©2013 / BookDesignTemplates.com
Edited by Ann Bartz / WritingSolved.com

Printed in the United States of America
First Printing, 2015

ISBN 978-0-9968854-0-9 (EPUB)

ISBN 978-0-9968854-1-6 (Paperback)

ISBN 978-0-9968854-2-3 (Audiobook)

Books may be purchased in quantity and/or special sales by contacting the publisher:

Monarch Unlimited
20555 Devonshire St. #373,
Chatsworth, CA 91311

by phone 818-923-6000, by fax 818-923-6001, or by email at Sales@MonarchUnlimited.us.

*For my father, in honor of
the 100th anniversary of his birth.*

Nathan D. Whitney
1915-2009

Acknowledgments

Thank you to the following individuals, without whose support, inspiration, and contributions to my knowledge, as well as other help, this book would not have been written:

> Ed Ward, Carolyn Ward, Blake Crawford,
> Nathan B. Whitney, Ryan Mendenhall,
> Kamal Ravikant, Nick Usborne, Tim Grahl
> Robert Rose, Valerie Vagoda, Tania Getty

And special acknowledgement to Anthony Robbins, who introduced this book to me and whose teachings have made an enormous difference in my life.

Finally, to my inspiring, loving, and supportive soul mate, Tonya Foster: my deepest gratitude. Your encouragement from the beginning—and at every step along the way—is greatly appreciated. It was such a comfort and relief to know that you were always there. Not to mention your giving birth to our son in the middle of it all. I offer you my most heartfelt thanks.

Contents

CHARACTER 1

CIRCUMSTANCES 7

HEALTH AND BODY 21

PURPOSE 27

ACHIEVEMENT 33

VISIONS AND IDEALS 39

SERENITY 47

We don't see things as they are, we see them as we are.

—ANAIS NIN

Introduction

This book started as an exercise. I simply wanted to better understand the writing of James Allen in his seminal work, *As a Man Thinketh*, originally published in 1902. I struggled with the dated material. Some references and sensibilities from that period muddied the message, and I often found myself asking what he meant and how it was relevant today. I needed clarity. While looking up definitions and researching references, I began to rewrite phrases, then sentences, paragraphs, and eventually entire chapters.

As the exercise turned into this book, it became a much more cathartic experience than I expected. It made me question my limitations and tested my beliefs. To gain the understanding I sought, I had to challenge what I had previously thought about positive thinking and the Law of Attraction. And when I inadvertently deleted the first draft, I had to dig down deep inside myself to discover how much I needed to complete this project—and start over.

The end of the nineteenth century was the beginning of the New Thought movement. People started articulating theories about the power of the mind and how thoughts influence the physical world. Before there were terms for "positive thinking" and "Law of Attraction" there were the originators of these concepts. I found that in going back to the beginning, you discover some things that have been lost along the way.

For James Allen, the power of thought is about much more than positive thinking—and is not at all about attracting what you want. He believed that the evolution of our thoughts determines who we are, how we will change, and whether or not we achieve our goals.

There are significant distinctions between what James Allen wrote in 1902 and more contemporary works, like Rhonda Byrne's 2006 blockbuster hit, *The Secret*. Something had gone awry in modern nomenclature, and what I discovered in *As a Man Thinketh* makes all the difference.

One of the most significant revelations was how James Allen perceived the principle of attraction. Working on this adaptation helped me learn what it really takes to manifest your deepest desires and fulfill the destiny of your choosing.

Beyond illuminating the core principles of New Thought, *As a Man Thinketh* transcends its own time, as well as the past one hundred years. And not only does it remain relevant today, its resonance will grow even deeper as the practice of mindfulness becomes more prevalent.

For those who are familiar with this subject, you have an opportunity to challenge your preconceived notions. For uninitiated readers, this is your chance to approach a cornerstone treatise from the New Thought movement in an accessible and contemporary context. For every reader, there is insight on how to improve your life and put the power of your own thoughts to work for you.

This adaptation is my take on *As a Man Thinketh*. The philosophy is all James Allen's. What I have done is contemporize much of the language, update references, rephrase and elaborate on some concepts, and add context.

I am grateful for the opportunity to share this work with you. I hope you enjoy reading the wisdom of *As a Man Thinketh* as I came to understand it. Think what you want.

> Mind is the Master-power that molds and makes,
>
> And Man is Mind, and evermore he takes
>
> The tool of Thought, and, shaping what he wills
>
> Brings forth a thousand joys, a thousand ills:--
>
> He thinks in secret, and it comes to pass:
>
> Environment is but his looking-glass
>
> —JAMES ALLEN

Foreword

As a Man Thinketh

This little volume (the result of meditation and experience) is not intended as an exhaustive treatise on the much-written-upon subject of the power of thought. It is suggestive rather than explanatory, its object being to stimulate men and women to the discovery and perception of the truth that:

They themselves are makers of themselves

by virtue of the thoughts which they choose and encourage; that mind is the master-weaver, both of the inner garment of character and the outer garment of circumstance, and that, as they may have hitherto woven in ignorance and pain they may now weave in enlightenment and happiness.

—JAMES ALLEN

CHAPTER ONE

CHARACTER

A man's life is what his thoughts make of it.

— MARCUS AURELIUS

"For as a man thinketh in his heart, so is he." Taken from the Biblical passage Proverbs 23:7, this quote is part of a cautionary tale that introduces the central concept of this book—that a person's thoughts are so pervasive they define the entirety of his life and character. So much so that no matter what appearances may be, a person cannot escape from who he truly is. Your character is the sum total of all your thoughts. And by extension, every condition and circumstance of your life is a direct result of the thoughts that make you who and what you are. We are all literally *what we think*.

Just as every living plant grows from—and could not even exist without—its seed, every act by a person stems from the seeds of their thoughts. Whether you are conscious of these thoughts or they are hidden in your subconscious, your actions would not exist without them. This applies equally to all actions whether they are spontaneous and "unpremeditated" or you execute them deliberately.

Every act is the blossom of thought, the fruits of which can range from joy to misery. You garner both the sweet and bitter harvest of the thoughts you cultivate.

Man develops the same as every living creature: in accordance with the laws of nature. We are not a creation of any artifice, no matter how clever or cunning. The principles of cause and effect are as absolute and undeviating in the realm of conscious and subconscious thought as they are in the physical world.

A noble and joyful character is not a thing of favor or chance. It is the natural result of continuous effort in determined thinking. It is the effect of long-cherished associations with positive thoughts. An ignoble and slovenly character, by the same process, results from the harboring of groveling thoughts.

Man is made or unmade by himself. Your own thoughts forge the weapons that can bring about your destruction. Conversely, you fashion the tools with which to create a magnificent life of joy, peace, and abundance. By making constructive choices in the true application of positive thinking you can ascend to unimaginable heights. But by abusing yourself with negative thoughts, you will descend to depths of despair. Between these two extremes are every variety of character and circumstance for which we are the makers and masters of our own selves.

Of all the remarkable insights pertaining to the human mind, none is more enlightening and filled with unquestionable promise than the realization of man as the master of thought, the molder of character and maker of conditions that shape the circumstances that lead to his own destiny.

As master of your own thoughts, you hold the key to every situation, and contain within yourself the power of intelligence and faculty for love to regenerate and transform your life. You can make of yourself all that you have the will to do.

Man is always the master—even in his weakest and most degenerative state. Out of weakness and abandon, man becomes a foolish master who misleads his life. But when you begin to reflect on your circumstances and search diligently for the truth about your condition, you will grow to be a wise master.

Direct your energies with deliberate intention and focus your thoughts on positive outcomes. Such is the nature of a *conscious* master. You can raise your consciousness only by discovering—*within yourself*—the power of your own thoughts. This discovery process is totally a matter of application, self-analysis, and experience.

Only through dedicated exploring and mining are gold and gemstones discovered. You can find every truth connecting the circumstances of your life if you dig deep into the mine of your very being and discover for yourself how you are the maker of your character, molder of your life, and builder of your destiny. As you observe, control, and alter your thoughts—tracing their effects on yourself, on others, and on the circumstances of your life—you will unerringly find the link between the cause and effect of your thoughts.

With patient practice and investigation into your every experience, down to the most trivial everyday occurrence—in an effort to obtain such knowledge of yourself—you will discover understanding, wisdom, and power. Through this process, as in no other, will you comprehend the significance of ancient teachings like those of the Biblical Matthew, "He who asks shall receive, the one who seeks shall find; and to him that knocks, the door shall be opened." It is only through enduring patience, relentless practice, and ceaseless persistence that you will unlock the door of knowledge and enter the world of opportunity.

> Thought in the mind hath made us. What we are
>
> By thought we wrought and built. If a man's mind
>
> Hath evil thoughts, pain comes on him as comes
>
> The wheel behind the ox… If one endure
>
> In purity of thought, joy follows him
>
> As his own shadow—sure.
>
> —JAMES ALLEN

CHAPTER TWO

CIRCUMSTANCES

People are always blaming their circumstances for what they are. I don't believe in circumstances. The people who get on in this world are the people who get up and look for the circumstances they want, and if they can't find them, make them.

— GEORGE BERNARD SHAW

Think of your mind as a garden. That garden may be intelligently cultivated or allowed to run thoughtlessly wild. Regardless of whether you cultivate it or neglect it, it must—and it will—grow accordingly. If you do not consciously put useful seeds into the garden, then useless seeds will mindlessly fall into it and produce an abundance of undesirable results.

Just as a gardener cultivates his plot, keeps it free of weeds, and grows the flowers and fruits he desires, so must man tend the garden of his mind. You can weed out all the negative, useless, and counterproductive thoughts and cultivate the fruits of your desires with positive, useful, and productive thoughts. Through intentional pursuit of this process you will discover—sooner or later—that you are the "master gardener" of your mind and the director of your life. As you dig deeper into your thoughts, your understanding of their cause and effect will grow. You will discover, with ever-increasing frequency, how the power of thought and workings of your mind operate in the shaping of your character, circumstances, and destiny.

Thought and character are inseparable. But you can discover character only as it manifests itself through environment and circumstance. The outer conditions of a man's life will always be harmoniously related to his inner state of mind. This does not mean that his circumstances, at any given moment, are a reflection of a person's entire character overall. But those circumstances are so intimately connected to some vital thought pattern within, that they are indispensable to his development for that moment in time.

Every one of us is where we are in accordance with our own state of being. The thoughts that you build your life upon lead you to where you are. As to the arrangement of your circumstances, there is no element of chance. Everything in your life is the result of a process that err.

This is just as true for those who feel "out of harmony" with their surroundings as it is for those who are content with them. If you feel yourself in the "wrong situation" you need to find a way out. You need to tend the garden of your mind—weed out the corrupting thoughts and nurture the fruitful ones.

As a consciously developing being, you have an opportunity to learn in every situation you find yourself—so that you may grow. As you learn the integral lessons that every situation holds for you, current circumstances will give way to others that offer you new opportunities to grow.

Man is controlled by circumstances so long as he believes himself to be a product of external forces and outside conditions. Once you realize you are a creative force of your own and you control the nature of your being—from which each situation grows—then you will master the life you lead.

Circumstances are nothing but the result of the thoughts that create them. As you practice thoughtfulness and self-discipline over time, this will become readily evident. You will notice that changes to your situation happen in direct relation to changes in your mental process. In fact, the more earnestly you dedicate yourself to cultivating the nature of your thoughts, the more swiftly changes will come, and you will pass rapidly through a succession of transformations.

Everything you think, feel, and do—consciously or subconsciously—determines what you will attract. What you attract depends on the thoughts that you harbor deep-down inside yourself. This applies to that which you most desire and to that which you most fear. This is what enables you to reach the height of your most cherished aspirations, or drags you down to the depths of your most abhorrent nightmare. Circumstances you find yourself in are the means by which you receive that which you attract. Think what you want.

Your every thought springs from seeds you intentionally sow or from seeds you allow to take root out of neglect. These thoughts will continue to grow and blossom into action. Sooner or later they will enable you to seize the opportunity in any given situation. Positive thoughts will lead to desired results and negative thoughts will deliver undesirable consequences.

As the reaper of his own harvest, man learns just as much from inhospitable conditions as from favorable ones. Your innermost thoughts shape the circumstances you find yourself in. Both the pleasant and unpleasant conditions of those situations factor equally into your ultimate good.

In following your innermost desires, aspirations, and dreams, you choose which ones will dominate your thoughts. Whether you end up languishing in fantasies and daydreams or steadfastly pursuing your greatest endeavors, you will ultimately reap what you sow.

In physics, the principle of attraction refers to motion. Bodies moving in the same direction attract. Bodies moving in opposite directions repel. In life, you will attract only that which is in alignment with the direction you choose to take.

A man does not fall into a life of crime by the tyranny of fate or happenstance, but by a pathway he has chosen with abject thoughts and base desires. Nor does a good-hearted man fall suddenly into corruption by way of stress or some outside pressure. The corrupting thoughts have long been fostered by his deepest desires. His true character revealed itself only by seizing the opportunity he had long sought.

Circumstance does not make the man. Circumstance reveals a man's true character to himself. No conditions can exist that compel a man into vice and its attendant sufferings apart from his own deviant inclinations. Likewise, a man cannot attain peace and happiness without continuous cultivation of edifying aspirations.

As ruler of his own thoughts, man makes of himself what he draws from opportunity. Opportunities spring from the environment he leads himself into.

From the moment you are born, your every act is to attract those combinations of conditions that create the results you desire. And at every stage of your development you reveal yourself by your actions—good and bad. Your character is reflected by the strengths and weaknesses you display at each turn of events.

You do not attract that which you *want*, but from which you *are*. You may find your whims, fancies, and ambitions thwarted at every step. But your innermost thoughts and desires are being fulfilled, whether fair or foul and whether you realize it or not. The true nature of what shapes our destiny is within ourselves. It is our very self.

Man is shackled only by himself. If you allow your thoughts and actions to be the jailers of your fate, you will be imprisoned by your own destructive thinking. Alternately, your thoughts and actions can be wings of freedom. You can be liberated by virtue of your own positive thinking.

A man does not simply get what he wishes and dreams for, but receives that which he has wrought. You realize your dreams and wishes only when they harmonize with your thoughts and actions. If you find yourself at odds with your circumstances and are continually struggling to change them, it's because you are revolting against an *effect,* instead of tending to the *cause* that produced it deep inside yourself.

That cause may take the form of a conscious vice or an unconscious weakness. But whatever the cause may be, it is the source of your impediment and falls upon you to remedy.

People who are anxious to improve their circumstances, but unwilling to improve themselves, will remain trapped. The person who is dedicated to self-improvement can never fail to accomplish what he has his heart on—if he is willing to change his thoughts and behavior. This is as true for material ambitions as it is for spiritual quests. A person whose sole ambition is to acquire wealth must be prepared to make great personal sacrifices to accomplish his goal. Even more so must someone devoted to realizing a life of complete spiritual well-being.

Think of a man who is wretchedly unhappy—someone who is extremely anxious that his circumstances and living conditions should be better. Yet this man shirks his work and feels justified in trying to deceive his employer because he is underpaid. Such a man does not understand the simplest and most rudimentary principles upon which success is built. Not only is he totally unfit to rise out of his misery, but also he is actually attracting to himself even more wretchedness by dwelling in and acting out indolent, deceptive, and negative thoughts.

Now think of a rich man—someone who suffers a painful and persistent disease as a result of his own gluttony. He is willing to give large sums of money for treatment. But he will not sacrifice his gluttonous behavior. He wants to gratify his desire for rich and opulent indulgences and have his health, too. Such a man is wholly unfit for health because he has not learned even the basic principles of healthy living.

What of an employer who adopts crooked measures to avoid paying proper wages and—in an effort to make higher profits—provides dangerous working conditions for his employees? Such a man is altogether unfit for prosperity. And when he finds himself bankrupt, in both reputation and riches, he will blame outside influences for his circumstances and take no responsibility for his role as sole author of his own condition.

These are just three examples that illustrate how man is the cause (nearly always unconsciously) of his own circumstances. Even with every intention of achieving positive results, we are continually frustrating ourselves with thoughts and desires that cannot possibly harmonize with our objectives. There are myriad examples that could be multiplied and varied almost indefinitely. But it's much more important for you to understand the power of your own thoughts in the cause and effect on your life, actions, and circumstances. Once resolved to comprehend this, you will discover how external factors cannot serve as the source for your condition—whether you like it or not.

Individual circumstances are complicated. Thoughts are deeply rooted. Conditions for happiness vary greatly. Perhaps known only to himself, the truth of a man's overall condition cannot be judged by another based solely on observations of outward appearances.

A person may appear honest in certain regards, yet they suffer in deprivation. Another may appear dishonest in certain regards, yet they enjoy every advantage. But to draw a conclusion that one fails *because of his particular honesty* or the other succeeds *because of her particular dishonesty* is nothing more than superficial judgment. You cannot assume that the dishonest person is totally corrupt or that the honest one is entirely virtuous. A deeper knowledge and broader understanding of a person's experience would render such superficial judgments erroneous.

A seemingly dishonest person may have admirable virtues you did not know she possessed. An apparently honest person may harbor depraved vices you could not have discerned. The honest person reaps the rewards of his positive thoughts and actions just as much as he brings upon himself the sufferings produced by his depravity. It is, likewise, the same for the dishonest person. Appearances can be deceiving. Passing judgment on others is an exercise in futility.

There can be a certain reassurance in believing one suffers due to one's virtues. But not until you have utterly removed every shred of vain, bitter, and negative thought from your mind and come clean for every wrong you ever committed could you be in a position to truly know—and assuredly declare—that your sufferings are the result of your positive intentions and not your negative thoughts. A journey toward such sublime insight into the workings of your mind and life would reveal—in no uncertain terms—that you cannot derive good from evil or evil from good.

Positive thoughts and affirmative actions cannot produce poor results. Negative thoughts and antagonizing actions cannot produce good results. This is the same as saying, "Nothing can come from corn but corn, and nothing from weeds but weeds." We can easily understand the laws of nature as they apply to the physical world. But it's more difficult to understand that the same laws apply to the unseen world of thought and energy (though their application is just as true and undeviating). In failing to comprehend this, you will fail to benefit from it.

Suffering is *always* the result of negative thought in some regard. It is an indication that an individual is out of harmony with herself and the true state of her being. There is, however, a supreme purpose for this suffering. You can use it to reveal all that is useless and negative and burn it out. For him who lives his life in harmony with himself, suffering ends. There is no point in continuing to burn down gold after the impurities have been removed. Neither could a perfectly enlightened soul continue to suffer.

The circumstances a person encounters through suffering are the result of his own internal disharmony. The situations another encounters through joy are the result of her harmonious alignment of thought and action. Joy is the measure of positive thinking, not material rewards. Wretchedness is the measure of negative thinking, not the lack of material rewards. Someone may be wretched and rich, or joyful and poor. Happiness and wealth join together only when wealth is gained justly and used wisely. An impoverished man descends into wretchedness only when he blames his predicament on a burden unjustly imposed upon him.

Indigence and indulgence are two extremes of wretchedness. Both are equally undesirable and the result of disharmony. You cannot be happy, healthy, and prosperous unless your thoughts are in harmony with your actions. Happiness, health, and prosperity are the result of aligning your inner self with your outward behavior.

A man begins to be whole only when he ceases to whine and rail against his current predicament and starts searching for the true forces that govern his life. As he adapts his thinking around these governing forces, he will stop accusing others as the source of his condition. The more you strengthen yourself by the power of your own thoughts, the less you will fight against your circumstances and begin to build upon them as a means of discovering the hidden possibilities within yourself.

The dominating principles of the laws that govern the universe create order, not chaos. Creation and procreation are the substance of life. Destruction is not. Virtue over corruption is the quest of spiritual enlightenment. Each process adheres to the motivating forces that drive it. Likewise, your every action is aligned with motivating forces throughout the universe. The process of aligning your motivations with your desires will attract that which is similarly motivated. As you alter your thinking to match your motivation and drive you toward the things and people you want to attract, those very things and people will be attracted to you in kind.

The proof of this can be readily determined by anyone willing to investigate through systematic introspection and self-analysis. If you radically alter your thoughts, you will be astonished at the rapid transformation you elicit on the conditions of your life.

People imagine that thought can be kept secret—but it cannot. Thought manifests itself as habit. And habit creates circumstance. Base thoughts materialize as habits of intemperance and debauchery that result in self-destructive and debilitating circumstances. Indulgent thoughts of every kind lead to enervating and unstable habits that leave you in disorienting and adverse predicaments. Thoughts of fear, doubt, and indecision produce feeble, unproductive, and insecure habits that ultimately lead to circumstances of failure, indigence, and co-dependency. Apathetic thoughts result in slovenly and shiftless habits that lead to foul and destitute predicaments. Thoughts of hatefulness and condemnation produce recriminating and violent habits that end in situations of suffering and persecution. All thoughts of self-indulgence lead to habits that result in dissatisfying circumstances.

On the other hand, beautiful thoughts of every variety create habits of gratitude and kindness that lead to pleasant and uplifting conditions. Peaceful thoughts create habits of temperance and good will that result in circumstances of ease and tranquility. Thoughts of courage, self-reliance, and decisiveness create bold habits that lead to situations of success, independence, and accomplishment. Productive thoughts create habits of organization and industry that result in conditions of stability and prosperity. Gentle and forgiving thoughts create habits of tenderness that lead to circumstances of preservation and sanctuary. Loving and unselfish thoughts create habits of selflessness that lead to a world of abiding serenity and enduring abundance.

Persisting in any given train of thought—be it good or bad—cannot fail to produce its results upon character and circumstance, accordingly. While you cannot *directly* choose your conditions, you can choose your thoughts. The thoughts you choose indirectly—yet surely—shape your circumstances.

The laws of cause and effect determine the degree of gratification you receive. According to the thoughts you most encourage, you will encounter the opportunities that most readily manifest from both good and evil intentions, equally.

If you cease your negative thoughts, a world of possibilities will open up and be ready to help you. If you put away your weak and sickly thoughts, endless opportunities will present themselves at every turn to aid in your determined resolve. If you encourage positive thoughts, no hard fate can bind you down in wretchedness and shame. The world is your kaleidoscope, and the varying combinations of opportunities you discover at every succeeding moment present to you the exquisitely adjusted results of your ever-evolving thoughts.

> You will be what you will to be;
>
> Let failure find its false content
>
> In that poor word, "environment,"
>
> But spirit scorns it, and is free.
>
>
> It masters time, it conquers space;
>
> It cows that boastful trickster, Chance,
>
> And bids the tyrant Circumstance
>
> Uncrown, and fill a servant's place.

> The human Will, that force unseen,
>
> The offspring of a deathless Soul,
>
> Can hew a way to any goal,
>
> Though walls of granite intervene.
>
> Be not impatient in delay,
>
> But wait as one who understands;
>
> When spirit rises and commands,
>
> The gods are ready to obey.
>
> —JAMES ALLEN

CHAPTER THREE

HEALTH AND BODY

The root of all health is in the brain. The trunk of it is in emotion. The branches and leaves are the body. The flower of health blooms when all parts work together.

— KURDISH SAYING

The body is the servant of the mind. It responds to signals from the brain and obediently follows all instructions from the mind, whether they be conscious decisions or involuntary commands. In response to slovenly thoughts, the body readily sinks into disease and decay. Positive and uplifting thoughts, however, invigorate the body with youthfulness and beauty.

Like external circumstances, internal conditions of disease and health are rooted in thought. Sickly thoughts will express themselves through a sickly body. Thoughts of fear can kill a man as readily as a bullet or, less rapidly, through a plague of continual thoughts of dread. The people who live in fear of disease are the people who get it. Anxiety debilitates the whole body, lays it open and leaves it vulnerable to disease. Thoughts of self-destructive behavior, even if not physically indulged in, are just as capable of ravaging your nervous system.

Strong, wholesome, and positive thoughts strengthen the body with vigor and verve. Your body is a delicate and malleable instrument that responds eagerly to the thoughts impressed upon it. The habits you create from your thoughts will have their own impact on your body—for better or worse.

People will continue to suffer ravages of the body and poisoned blood so long as they propagate negative thoughts. Out of a clear mind comes a healthy life and clean body. Out of a defiled mind comes a corrupt life and diseased body. Thought is the wellspring of action and manifestation in your life. Keep the fountainhead primed and all will flow cleanly.

A change of diet will not help people who will not change their thinking. When a man keeps his focus on healthy thoughts, he will no longer desire unhealthy food.

If you want to strengthen your body, guard your mind. If you want to rejuvenate your body, invigorate your mind. Thoughts of malice, envy, discouragement, and gloom rob the body of its health and beauty. A sour face does not come by chance—it is wrought from sour thoughts. Unwanted wrinkles are drawn from indulgence, scorn, and pride.

A woman of 96 may have the bright and innocent face of youth, while a man well under middle-age can have a face drawn into incongruous contours. One is the result of a healthy and sunny disposition. The other is the outcome of bitterness and discontent.

Just as you cannot have a clean and wholesome home unless you admit fresh air and sunshine freely into your rooms, a strong body and vibrant or serene countenance can result only from freely admitting into your mind uplifting thoughts of gratitude, good will, and abundance.

On the faces of the elderly, you will find many types of wrinkles. Some are formed from kindliness, others by strong and determined thoughts. Some are carved by bitterness. Who cannot distinguish them? With those who have lived wholesomely, age is calm, peaceful, and softly mellowed like the setting sun. I remember my father on his deathbed. He was not old, except in years. He died as sweetly and peacefully as he had lived.

There is no physician like cheerful thoughts to dispel the ills of the body. There is no comforter to compare with good will for alleviating the pain of grief and sorrow. To live continually in thoughts of ill will, cynicism, suspicion, and envy is to be confined to a self-made prison cell. But to think well of others, to be positive in every event, and to patiently seek out the good will in all are the selfless thoughts that lead the way toward enlightenment.

> ...to dwell day by day in thoughts of peace toward every creature will bring abounding peace to their possessor.
>
> —JAMES ALLEN

CHAPTER FOUR

PURPOSE

A human being with a settled purpose must accomplish it, and nothing can resist a will that will stake even existence for its fulfillment.

— DISRAELI

Until you focus your thoughts on a specific purpose, there can be no exceptional accomplishment. For most people, rudderless thoughts allow them to drift aimlessly on the ocean of life. Aimlessness is a transgression as much as any vice. You cannot allow yourself to drift through life if you want to steer clear of catastrophe and ruin.

If you have no central purpose in life, you will easily fall prey to petty worries, fears, troubles, and self-pity. All of which lead surely—as if deliberately planned—to incapacity, unhappiness, and defeat. In an evolving universe driven by the ability to adapt, uncertainty leads only to irrelevancy.

Conceive a genuine purpose that is true to your heart. Make this purpose the central focus of your thoughts. It may take the form of a spiritual ideal or a worldly object. But whatever it is, find something meaningful to you and steadily fix your every thought upon the goal you set before you.

Make this purpose your paramount duty and devote yourself unyieldingly to attaining it. The definitive pathway of self-discipline ultimately leads to manifestation of thought. Do not let your thoughts wander into passing fancies, distractions, or daydreams. Even if you fail again and again (as you necessarily must to overcome challenges), the *strength of character you gain* will be the true measure of your success. Each time you start over, you will be better poised at every turn for the next endeavor and for ever-greater triumphs.

For those who are not prepared for the daunting quest of a *great purpose*, fix your thoughts on the impeccable performance of your work, no matter how insignificant a task may seem. In this way you can gather your thoughts, find focus, and develop the strength of resolve. Once you do that, you will discover there is nothing that you cannot accomplished.

Even the most reticent, the most cautious, and the most uncertain among us must recognize their own weaknesses and remember this: *Strength can be developed only by effort and practice.* Allow this to empower you and simply add effort to effort, patience to patience, and strength to strength. In so doing, you will never stop developing. You will increasingly gain the strength of resolve.

Just as a physically weak person can build strength through careful and patient training, someone of little willpower can build mental determination by exercising his power of thought.

By putting aside aimless and wandering thoughts and beginning to think with purpose, you will join the ranks of those who see failure as merely an inevitable step on the pathway to success. Those who make the most of every circumstance, who think boldly and attempt fearlessly, will accomplish masterfully.

Once you have conceived a purpose, you should plan out in your mind a *straight and narrow* course for achieving it. Do not let your thoughts wander in any direction and do not waiver from this course. Doubts and fears must be rigorously rejected. They are degenerate influences that derail the steadfast course of effort and render your plan corrupt, ineffectual, and useless. Thoughts of doubt and fear cannot accomplish *anything* and never will. They will guarantee your doom. Purpose, effort, willpower, and focused thoughts are all debilitated when doubt and fear creep into your thoughts.

Thought, fearlessly committed to purpose, becomes a creative force. Once you truly *know* this, you'll be ready to become something much greater and much, much more than a jumble of meandering thoughts and fleeting desires. And once you actually *do* this, you'll become the ruler of your own thoughts and master of your own destiny.

> The will to do springs from the knowledge that we can do. Doubt and fear are the great enemies of knowledge, and he who encourages them, who does not slay them, thwarts himself at every step.
>
> He who has conquered doubt and fear has conquered failure. His every thought is allied with power, and all difficulties are bravely met and wisely overcome.
>
> His purposes are seasonably planted, and they bloom and bring forth fruit which does not fall prematurely to the ground.
>
> —JAMES ALLEN

CHAPTER FIVE

ACHIEVEMENT

Act as though it were impossible to fail.

— DOROTHEA BRANDE

Everything you achieve and everything you fail to achieve are direct results of your own thoughts. In a universe governed by the laws of physics, there is equilibrium between positive and negative forces. Loss of balance in the order of things would lead to total chaos.

Responsibility for your individual role must be absolute. Your weakness and strength, sincerity and incredulity are of your own making and not anyone else's. And since they are brought about by your own self and no other, only you can change them, and absolutely no other.

Your circumstances are also yours alone and not due to someone else. All your sufferings and happiness are derived from within you. As you think, so you are. As you continue to think, so you will remain the same. As you change your thinking, so you will change.

A strong person cannot help a weaker one, unless the weak one is *willing* to be helped. And even then, the weak one must gain strength on his own and by his own efforts. He must develop in himself the strength he admires in another. No one but yourself can change you.

Conventional wisdom would say, "If people are downtrodden, it's because someone else is an oppressor. Let us hate the oppressor." Then there are those who would say, "One man is an oppressor because so many people are downtrodden. Let us hate the oppressed." The truth is, the oppressor, and the oppressed are co-conspirators in ignorance. While it seems that one afflicts the other, the reality is that each afflicts only themselves.

From this perspective, it is possible to perceive how the actions of the oppressed serve to continue their own oppression just as much as the oppressor misapplies power in continuing to oppress them. Through love, the suffering inherent in both states is revealed and condemns neither. True compassion embraces both the oppressor and the oppressed.

She who has mastered her thoughts will have learned to put away all selfishness and fear. She belongs to neither oppressor nor oppressed. She is truly free.

You can rise up, conquer fear and achieve goals only by owning your thoughts. You can remain weak, abject, and miserable only by refusing to own up to your thoughts.

Before you can achieve anything, even worldly things, you must focus your thoughts beyond immediate gratification and selfish indulgences. Of course, to succeed you don't have to give up all joy and pleasure. But you do need to make certain sacrifices. If you were consumed with immediate gratification, how could you think clearly or plan methodically? You would not be able to find opportunities or develop resources and would fail at any significant undertaking. If you don't master your thoughts, you will be in no position to control affairs and adopt serious responsibilities. You would not be fit to act independently and stand on your own. But you are limited only by the thoughts you choose.

You cannot make much progress, let alone achieve anything, without sacrifice. Your ability to succeed will be measured by the sacrifices you make. By forgoing instant gratification and fleeting fancies, you will be able to fully focus your mind on developing your plans, strengthening your resolve, and building self-discipline. The more you focus your thoughts, the stronger your will becomes, the greater your success will be. And the greater your success, the more enduring will be your achievements.

The universe does not favor the greedy, the dishonest, or the vicious—even though it may sometimes appear that way. The universe does attune for the honest, the magnanimous and the pure of heart. Throughout the ages, and to varying degrees, all the great teachers have agreed on this. If you want to prove it and learn this for yourself, all you have to do is persist in committing fully to pure intentions through clear and focused thought.

Intellectual achievements are the result of thought devoted to seeking knowledge, truth, or beauty in the physical world. And though some achievements may be rife with vanity or blind ambition, they are not wrought from such characteristics. They are the inevitable results of long and arduous effort through focused and selfless thought.

Spiritual achievements are attained through transcendent fervor. Those who live constantly in the realm of enlightened and loving thought—who dwell only upon what is pure and unselfish—will become wise and peaceful in character. Just as surely as the sun will rise and the moon will grow full, they will gain prominence, influence, and reverence.

Achievement of any kind is the dividend of persistent effort and focused thought. Through self-discipline, resolution, veracity, devotion, and thoroughly sincere intentions, you will reach great heights. But wallow in indulgence, indolence, delusion, deception, and scattered thinking, and you will sink to lowly depths.

You can attain worldly success of great measure and even sanctity in the spiritual realm. But at any time, you can succumb to corruption and wretchedness by allowing arrogant, greedy, and self-serving thoughts to take root.

Triumphs of achievement attained through committed thought and concerted effort can be sustained only by mindful vigilance. It is so very easy to slip up once success is in your grasp. It is surprising how rapidly you can fall back into ineffectual malaise.

> All achievements, whether in the business, intellectual, or spiritual world, are the result of definitely directed thought, are governed by the same law and are of the same method; the only difference lies in the object of attainment.
>
> He who would accomplish little must sacrifice little; he who would achieve much must sacrifice much; he who would attain highly must sacrifice greatly.
>
> —JAMES ALLEN

CHAPTER SIX

VISIONS AND IDEALS

Is it so bad, then, to be misunderstood? Pythagoras was misunderstood, and Socrates, and Jesus, and Luther, and Copernicus, and Galileo, and Newton, and every pure and wise spirit that ever took flesh. To be great is to be misunderstood.

— RALPH WALDO EMERSON

"Here's to the crazy ones," extolled Jack Kerouac. Dreamers are the saviors of this world. Just as the physical world is sustained by the invisible forces of nature, so too, are we. Through all our trials, tribulations and sordid affairs, our spirit is replenished by the astounding brilliance of those singular dreamers.

Humanity cannot forsake its dreamers. We cannot let their visions fade or die out. We thrive on their ideals. We know the dreamers' dreams by the *realities* they one day reveal and make manifest.

Composer, sculptor, painter, poet, prophet and sage—these are the designers of utopia and the architects of paradise. The world is beautiful because they have lived. Without them a toiling humanity would perish.

If you cherish a towering vision or a beautiful ideal with all your heart, you will one day realize it. William Wallace cherished a vision of independence and he achieved it. Copernicus formulated a vision of the universe and he revealed it. Buddha cherished the spiritual vision of a world made from pure enlightenment and he entered into it.

Cherish your visions. Cherish your ideals. Cherish the music that fills your heart. From the beauty that forms in your mind and the loveliness that fills your purest thoughts will come many delightful results and joyful returns. If you remain devoted to your cherished dreams, they will ultimately be made manifest.

Whether you desire physical gratification or aspire to great achievements, you will receive the fullest measure of that which you foster most rigorously. Ambitions that you do not focus your thoughts on will languish unfulfilled. That is how the Law of Attraction works. Everything you think prepares you for what circumstances will provide. No condition exists in which you "Ask and receive" what you do not believe.

If you are going to dream, dream big. Your dreams will lead you to what you will become. Your focus is the promise of what you will be. Your vision is the prophecy of what you will manifest.

The greatest of achievements started out as someone's dream. A mighty oak stems from the tiny acorn. From inside a cocoon, a caterpillar is transformed into a beautiful butterfly. Likewise, dreams are the seedlings of reality.

You may find yourself in unpleasant circumstances. But they don't need to stay that way. Just envision a goal and strive to reach it. The more you change yourself on the inside, the more you will change the circumstances around you. Picture a young adult, struggling in poverty, laboring for long hours, confined in an unhealthy work environment, uneducated and unskilled. But she dreams of a better life. She thinks about lofty ideals, refined craftsmanship, beautiful designs, and luxurious surroundings. She conceives in her mind and focuses her thoughts on visualizing her ideal life. Visions of having the freedom to do what she wants and living a grand lifestyle take possession of her. Unrest urges her into action. Soon, she spends all her spare time and whatever resources she can muster to improve her skills and develop herself.

Before long, her mindset will be altered so much that the familiar workplace will not be able to contain her. Her circumstances will have fallen so out of harmony with her thoughts that she can easily leave it all behind like an old sweater. Then, as new opportunities emerge, she recognizes them from an entirely new perspective and walks away from her past forever.

Years later, we'll see how this young adult has matured. As she continued to grow, she will have marshaled the forces of her thoughts with great mastery. She may wield influence upon the world stage with unequaled prowess. In her hands may lie enormous responsibilities. So much so that when she speaks, lives change. People seek out her advice and look to her for guidance in improving their circumstances. She may become a celebrated luminary around which innumerable destinies revolve. She can realize the vision of her youth. She can become one with her ideal self.

Each of us can realize the vision (not every passing fancy) that we hold most dear to our hearts. Whether your ideals are base, beautiful, or somewhere in between, you will gravitate toward that which you cherish most deeply. Life will deliver into your hands the exact results produced by your own thoughts.

You will receive only that which you sow—no more, no less. Whatever your current circumstances may be, you will fall down, stand still, or rise up with your thoughts, your vision, and your determination.

You control whether you'll become as small as your controlling vices, or as great as your dominant aspirations. In the words of Stanton Davis Kirkham:

> You may be keeping accounts, and

presently you shall walk out of the

door that for so long has seemed to you
the barrier of your ideals, and shall
find yourself before an audience - the
pen still behind your ear, the ink stains
on your fingers - and then and there shall
pour out the torrent of your inspiration.

You may be driving sheep, and you shall
wander to the city - bucolic and open
mouthed; shall wander under the intrepid
guidance of the spirit into the studio of
the master, and after a time he shall say,
'I have nothing more to teach you.' And now
you have become the master, who did so
recently dream of great things while driving
sheep. You shall lay down the saw and the
plane to take upon yourself the regeneration
of the world.

    Judging only by appearances, the thoughtless, the ignorant, and the indolent talk of "luck, fortune, and chance." Such people see someone grow rich and say, "Oh, how lucky they got!" When they encounter someone of great intellect, these people remark, "How privileged that one must be." And noting the esteem and influence garnered by another, they comment, "What a charmed life that person leads."

These detractors do not see the trials, the struggles, and the failures successful people have endured. They don't see what it takes to gain such experience. They don't know the sacrifices successful people have to make or the undaunted effort they have to exert. They don't understand the amount of faith successful people must exercise or how they must overcome the seemingly insurmountable to attain the goals envisaged in their hearts.

People who don't know the darkness of heartache see only the light of joy and call it "luck." People who don't see the long and arduous journey, but know only of the amazing achievement call it "good fortune." People who don't understand the process and perceive only the result call it "chance."

In all human endeavors there is *effort* and there are *results*. The determination of effort is the measure of a result. Chance is not. Status, power, material wealth, intellectual accomplishments, and spiritual rewards are the fruits of effort, the realization of comprehensive thoughts, the achievement of concrete goals, and the manifestation of vision.

> The Vision that you glorify in your mind, the Ideal that you enthrone in your heart – this you will build your life by, this you will become.
> —JAMES ALLEN

CHAPTER SEVEN

SERENITY

All that we are is the result of what we have thought:
it is founded on our thoughts and made up of our thoughts.

— GAUTAMA BUDDHA

Peace of mind is one of the prized jewels of wisdom. It is the result of long and patient effort in self-discipline. Its presence is an indication of seasoned experience, extraordinary knowledge of the laws of nature, and a complete understanding of the inner workings of thought.

You attain peace to the extent that you understand yourself to be a result of the evolution of your thoughts. Such knowledge necessitates, as well, the understanding of others as a product of their own thoughts. As you develop a deeper understanding and see more and more clearly the integral relationship between all things through the interaction of cause and effect, you will stop fussing and fuming with worry and fear. You will remain poised, steadfast, and serene.

The peaceful man, having learned how to govern himself, knows how to adapt himself to others. Others, in turn, revere his spiritual strength and feel calm. They feel that they can learn from him, trust him, and rely upon him. The more tranquil a man becomes the greater is his success, his influence, and his capacity to help others. Even an ordinary businessman will find his prosperity increases as he develops greater self-discipline and equanimity. People will always prefer to deal with someone whose demeanor is stable and even-tempered.

A composed and peaceful soul is loved and revered. Such a person is like a tree providing shade from the sweltering sun or a rock giving shelter in a storm. Who cannot admire a tranquil spirit, a sweet temperament, and a balanced life? It doesn't matter whether it rains or shines, or what challenges confront those possessing such blessings. They are always kind, serene, and peaceful.

That exquisite poise of character we call serenity is the pinnacle of self-awareness. It is the finest vintage of life. It is the blossoming of the soul. It is more precious than knowledge and more desirable than gold—than even the finest of luxury. How insignificant mere monetary gains seem in comparison with serene peace—a peace that dwells in the ocean of truth, beneath the waves, beyond the reach of tempests, and in a place of complete calm.

How many people do you know who poison their lives with bitterness, and ruin all that is sweet and beautiful with explosive tempers? They destroy their poise of character and create bad blood between themselves and others. It begs the question of whether the great majority of people ruin their lives and impede their own happiness by lack of self-control. How few people we meet in life who are well balanced, have that exquisite poise, and possess a serene character.

Yes, humanity surges with unbridled passions, tumults with unchecked fears, and is blown about by anxiety and doubt. Only through the harmony of focused thought and sincere effort can you calm the winds and storms brewing within and make them yield to your will.

> Tempest-tossed souls, wherever ye may be, under whatsoever conditions ye may live, know this – in the ocean of life the isles of Blessedness are smiling, and the sunny shore of your ideal awaits your coming.
>
> Keep your hand firmly upon the helm of thought. In the barque of your soul reclines the commanding Master; He does but sleep; wake Him. Self-control is strength; Right Thought is mastery; Calmness is power. Say unto your heart, "Peace, be still!"
>
> —JAMES ALLEN

ABOUT THE AUTHOR

Entrepreneur, speaker, and change agent Bruce Lee Whitney is an intrepid explorer of the tools, resources, and strategies that improve businesses and people's lives. After facing personal tragedy and professional challenges in 2009, Mr. Whitney applied his knowledge and experience in Change Management and Cognitive Behavioral Therapy to transform his life.

Since then he has dedicated himself to changing the lives of others, through the development of resources and training packages, executive and personal coaching, workshops, and speaking engagements. As founder and CEO of The Biggest Room of All, a transformative technology company in Los Angeles, he most recently developed the motivational app, **Affirmation Time,** for iOS and Android.

Before Mr. Whitney began his own journey of personal change, he worked with a diverse array of businesses—from the performing arts to technology and from corporations to startups. He placed each organization on a path to success by identifying where and how they needed to adapt to changing markets and changing times—and by helping the people within the organizations adapt to change, in order to improve. The inspiration for The Biggest Room of All comes from his signature greeting, "Welcome to the biggest room of all, the room for improvement!"

In addition to writing *Think What You Want*, Mr. Whitney is currently working on his forthcoming book, **Mindset, Ready, Go!** Please visit www.bruceleewhitney.com to learn more about the author.

www.ingramcontent.com/pod-product-compliance
Lightning Source LLC
Chambersburg PA
CBHW060429050426
42449CB00009B/2201